DiWALi BEDTiME STORiES

15 FASCINATING STORIES THAT WILL TAKE YOUR KID ON A MAGICAL JOURNEY TO THE WORLD OF DIWALI!

- Table of Content -

CHAPTER ONE

Ravi and the Firework Fiasco

Ravi is a mischievous little squirrel who lives inthe wonderful country of India. He has a heart as bright as the sun and a smile that can light up the universe. Ravi is very curious and this has led him into all sorts of adventures. As Diwali, the festival of lights, approached, the excitement in the air was palpable, and Ravi couldn't contain his curiosity.

Ravi's eyes sparkled with wonder and excitement as he watched all the animals in the forest prepare for Diwali. He watched as everyone took time decorating their homes with colorful rangoli and the most exciting part of it all for him was the beautiful lanterns they lit for the celebration. But one thing held Ravi's attention apart from the lit lanterns and that was the fireworks. The vibrant bursts of light in the night sky fascinated him.

One evening, unable to resist his curiosity any longer, Ravi decided to try his paw at setting off a small firework. He had seen others do it and was sure it would be harmless fun.

Ravi and the Firework Fiasco

Also, he didn't want to miss out on the festivities. Immediately Ravi lit the firework, it unexpectedly shot into the air with a loud bang, startling him and scattering sparks dangerously close to his friends' homes. He watched nervously as panic spread through the forest.All the animals scurried to protect their families and homes from the unexpected danger.

Ravi felt a pang of guilt for not learning how to light the firework and endangering his friends. He realized his mistake and knew he had to make things right. So, with the help of his friends, they quickly put out the small fires that the lit fireworks had created and ensured everyone was safe.

Once they were done, the wise old owl, Ollie, gathered all the forest animals and spoke about the importance of safety during Diwali. He explained that while Diwali was a time for celebration, it was equally crucial to be responsible and considerate of others.

Ravi felt deeply sorry for his actions and promised to be more careful in the future.

Ravi and the Firework Fiasco

He learned that Diwali was not just about fireworks and lights; it was about sharing joy, love, and kindness while being responsible for one another's safety.

From that day on, Ravi became the forest's safety ambassador during Diwali, making sure that everyone celebrated the festival responsibly. That night, as he looked up at the twinkling stars in the night sky, he knew that Diwali would always be a time of warmth, togetherness, and responsible celebration for him and his forest friends.

CHAPTER TWO

Lila and the Festival of Lights

Diwali always brings with it excitement and so as the days grew shorter and the air turned crisp, Lilabubbled like a pot of simmering sweetsin excitement. Every night, she would dream of Diwali and how she would celebrate it with her friends and family. She loved how the entire village came alive with vibrant colors and joyous celebrations and how all the children always gathered around to play. But more than anything, she loved the enchanting tradition of lighting diyas, little clay lamps, that adorned every home.

Lila's family had a special tradition they did every Diwali. They would spend hours together crafting intricate rangoli patterns at their doorstep. Everyone had a role to play during this, so Lila's job was to help her grandmother prepare delicious sweets, like crispy jalebis and fragrant gulab jamuns.

On the night of Diwali, just as Lila had looked forward to, the village square transformed into a magical wonderland.

Lila and the Festival of Lights

Countless diyas flickered, casting a warm glow over everything. The night sky lit up with bursts of colorful fireworks that painted the heavens, lighting up the faces of everyone in the village square.

Lila, like every other child in the village square, was amazed by the burst of colors and light.She loved how everyone was happy. For her, the most captivating part of Diwali was the story her grandmother told her each year. It was the story of the brave Prince Rama, his devoted wife Sita, and the loyal Hanuman. How they triumphed over darkness and returned home to a kingdom illuminated with countless lamps.

Lila always listened with rapt attention as her grandmother wove the tale of good conquering evil, of love and hope. Each year, as the story concluded, Lila would gaze at the diyas, her heart filled with a profound sense of joy and wonder.

Lila and the Festival of Lights

That night, as Lila snuggled under her soft blanket, her eyes sparkled with the reflection of the village's twinkling lights. She felt the warmth of Diwali in her heart, knowing that the festival was not just about lights but about spreading love, happiness, and the triumph of goodness.

With a smile on her face, Lila drifted into a peaceful slumber, her dreams filled with the radiant glow of the Festival of Lights, a timeless reminder of the power of light, love, and the joy of sharing with others.

CHAPTER THREE

The Magic Diyas of Diwali

Aarav jumped around in excitement. He couldn't seem to sit still for a whole minute. He was restless and would often walk to the calendar hanging in the hallway to count down how many days were left forDiwali. His favorite part of the festival was the magical diyas that his grandmother would light.

These were no ordinary diyas; they were "The Magic Diyas of Diwali." Legend had it that these diyas had the power to grant a single wish to anyone who lit them with a pure heart on Diwali night. Aarav wanted to make a wish and he sincerely hoped it would come true.

As the sun dipped below the horizon on Diwali eve, Aarav's grandmother gathered the family around. She handed Aarav a special diya, beautifully painted with vibrant colors and intricate designs. It was the Magic Diya.

The Magic Diyas of Diwali

With a heart full of hope, Aarav closed his eyes and made his wish. He wished for something that would bring happiness not only to him but to everyone in his village.

Carefully, he lit the Magic Diya. As its flame flickered to life, a warm, golden light filled the room. Aarav's heart skipped a beat. He felt a gentle breeze, and the flame danced in response.

Suddenly, he saw something truly magical. The room filled with the soft glow of countless diyas, all lit by his single Magic Diya. Aarav's wish had multiplied, spreading joy and light throughout the village.

As the night unfolded, Aarav's neighbors and friends visited, sharing stories and laughter. A sense of unity and happiness filled the air.

That night, as Aarav lay in bed, he knew he had witnessed something extraordinary.

The Magic Diyas of Diwali

The Magic Diyas had not just granted his wish but had shown him the true magic of Diwali – the magic of togetherness, kindness, and the joy of sharing.

With a contented heart, Aarav drifted into a peaceful slumber, the warm, golden light of the Magic Diyas still glowing in his dreams. And as he slept, the entire village twinkled with the light of love and unity, a gift from the enchanting Magic Diyas of Diwali.

CHAPTER FOUR

Mia's Diwali Delight

In a cozy little town, there lived a young girl named Mia who eagerly awaited the arrival of Diwali, the Festival of Lights, each year. Mia was known for her boundless curiosity and her wide-eyed wonder at the world around her.

As Diwali approached, Mia's excitement bubbled like the sweet syrup her mother made for jalebis. She loved watching the village come alive with color and light. She always loved to take a deep breath during this period as the air would be filled with the sweet aroma of traditional sweets, and everyone seemed to have a smile on their faces.

This year, Mia's heart was filled with a special longing. She wanted to do something extraordinary to make Diwali even more magical for her family and friends. Mia's grandmother noticed her restlessness and decided to share a story with her, a story of "Mia's Diwali Delight."

Mia's Diwali Delight

"Long ago," Mia's grandmother told her, "there was a young girl named Amara who lived in this very town. Like you, Amara adored Diwali. However, her family had faced hard times, and they couldn't afford to buy the beautiful clay lamps or sweets that others enjoyed during the festival."

"One year, just before Diwali, Amara decided to do something special. She gathered colorful leaves, twigs, and petals from the garden and created her decorations. With a heart full of love, she gave these homemade decorations to her family and friends."

"On Diwali night, as Amara's family lit the simple oil lamps, they noticed something magical. The light from their lamps seemed to dance and shimmer more brightly than ever before. Amara's love and creativity had infused these lamps with a special kind of magic."

Mia listened to this story in awe and this inspired her.She decided to create her own Diwali delight.

Mia's Diwali Delight

She spent days making handmade cards and personalized gifts for her loved ones. She poured her love and creativity into each one.

On Diwali night, as Mia's family and friends opened their gifts, they felt an overwhelming sense of love and joy. Mia's Diwali delight had worked its kind of magic, just like Amara's had.

Mia's heart swelled with happiness as she watched her loved ones smile and hug her tightly. She realized that the true magic of Diwali wasn't in the grandeur of the celebrations but in the love and thoughtfulness everyone shared.

That night, with a heart filled with contentment, Mia drifted off to sleep, her dreams illuminated by the warm, glowing memories of her Diwali delight. And as she slept, the village sparkled with the light of love and cherished moments, a gift from Mia to all those she held dear.

CHAPTER FIVE

Lila's Diwali Lantern

In a bustling forest, lived a curious and bright-eyed rabbit named Lila. Lila had always been fascinated by the stories her parents told her about Diwali, the festival of lights. The radiant glow of lanterns, the colorful rangoli, and the mouthwatering sweets filled her imagination with wonder.

That year, as Diwali approached, Lila's heart danced with excitement. She wanted to be a part of the festivities by finding the most magnificent lantern in the world. Determined to make her dreams come true, Lila hopped through the forest, searching high and low for the perfect lantern.

Her journey led her to the wise old tortoise, Guru Tilo, who was known for his wisdom and knowledge. Lila eagerly asked, "Guru Tilo, where can I find the most beautiful Diwali lantern?"

Lila's Diwali Lantern

Guru Tilo smiled gently and replied, "Dear Lila, the true beauty of Diwali is not found in extravagant lanterns but in the warmth and light that shines from within. Your heart, my dear, holds the key to the most beautiful light."

Confused but intrigued, Lila thanked Guru Tilo and continued her quest. She encountered fireflies, who shared their soft glow and stories of unity and happiness. Lila also met a kind grandmother who explained that Diwali was a time for family and friends to come together to share love and laughter.

After that encounter, Lila realized that the real light of Diwali was not in extravagant lanterns, but in the love, togetherness, and kindness that people shared. She returned to her meadow with a heart full of joy, realizing that the most beautiful lantern she could ever find was the one that shone from within her.

On the night of Diwali, Lila lit a simple lantern and watched it glow brightly, just like her heart.

Lila's Diwali Lantern

She knew that she had found the true essence of the festival, and as she looked at the starry sky, she whispered a thank you to Guru Tilo for teaching her that the real light of Diwali comes from within.

And so, in the meadow, surrounded by the beauty of simplicity and the warmth of her heart, Lila celebrated Diwali, spreading light, love, and happiness to all her forest friends. It was a Diwali they would never forget, all thanks to a curious rabbit who had learned that the most beautiful light shines from within.

CHAPTER SIX

The Sparkling Stories of Diwali

Every year, during the Diwali season, families in Chandrapur would gather around a bonfire the night before the festival. As the flames crackled and danced, a storyteller would step forward to share a tale of wonder and enchantment, and these stories became known as "The Sparkling Stories of Diwali."

One year, it was Aanya's turn to light the bonfire and share a story. Aanya has been looking forward to this all year long and couldn't wait to tell everyone her stories. Aanya was known for her vivid imagination, and everyone was eager to hear her tale.

She began, "Once upon a time, in a village much like ours, there lived a young boy named Aarav.Aarav loved Diwali more than anything in the world. His favorite part was the tradition of lighting diyas, the small clay lamps, and placing them along the riverbank. It was said that each diya carried a wish downstream, and if your heart's desire was pure, the river would carry it to the gods.

The Sparkling Stories of Diwali

One year, Aarav made a special wish. He wished for something that would bring happiness not only to him but to everyone in his village. With hope in his heart, he lit his diya and set it afloat on the gentle river.

That night, as Aarav slept, he had a dream. In his dream, he saw a brilliant, glowing diya rising from the river. It soared high into the night sky, illuminating the darkness with its radiant light.

The next morning, Aarav woke up and rushed to the riverbank. To his astonishment, he saw his diya glowing brilliantly, just as it had in his dream. But that wasn't all. The entire village was bathed in a warm, golden light.

Aarav's wish had come true, and the entire village was filled with joy and wonder. It was a Diwali like no other, and the memory of that night lived on in the hearts of the villagers.

The Sparkling Stories of Diwali

As Aanya finished her story, the bonfire crackled and sparkled. The villagers gazed at the flames, their hearts filled with the magic of "The Sparkling Stories of Diwali."

That night, as the children drifted off to sleep, their dreams were filled with the enchanting tales of Diwali and the hope that their own wishes would someday come true. And as they slept, the village was bathed in the warm, golden glow of love, unity, and the timeless tradition of "The Sparkling Stories of Diwali."

CHAPTER SEVEN

Diwali Wishes

Diwali is one of the most beloved celebrations in the village. It was also a time when the entire village came alive with happiness, laughter, vibrant colors, and radiant lights. The children in the village loved Diwali and cherished the moments they experienced but the most awaited moment of all was when they would all gather under the ancient banyan tree at the village square, known as the "Wish Tree."

Once gathered there, all the children would take turns to tie small, colorful pieces of cloth onto the branches of the tree, each containing a heartfelt wish written on it. They believed that the gods would read their wishes and grant them on the night of Diwali.

Amara was among the children and she happily stepped up on her toes to tie hers on the nearest branch to her.

Diwali Wishes

Amara was known for her big dreams and an even bigger heart. This Diwali, she had a special wish, one that she held close to her heart.

Amara's wish was to bring joy and happiness to her grandmother, who had been feeling lonely lately. She knew her grandmother missed the old Diwali celebrations with their extended family, and she wanted to make this year special for her.

On the night of Diwali, as the villagers gathered to light lamps and celebrate, something extraordinary happened. Amara's wish, along with all the wishes tied to the Wish Tree, twinkled with a soft, golden light. The villagers watched in amazement as the wishes seemed to come to life.

Amara's wish transformed into a radiant, golden butterfly. It fluttered gracefully through the air and landed gently on her grandmother's shoulder. Her grandmother smiled, feeling a warmth she hadn't felt in a long time.

Diwali Wishes

The entire village witnessed their wishes being granted in different ways, bringing joy and fulfillment to their hearts. Amara realized the true magic of Diwali was not just in making wishes but in the act of selflessly caring for others.

That night, as Amara lay in her cozy bed, she knew that Diwali wishes had the power to spread happiness far and wide. With a heart full of contentment, she drifted off to sleep, her dreams illuminated by the warm, golden light of "Diwali Wishes." As she and everyone slept, the village glowed with the light of love, unity, and the timeless tradition of making selfless wishes for others.

CHAPTER EIGHT

Riya and the Dancing Fireflies

In a peaceful village named SundarNagar, nestled amidst rolling hills and lush meadows, lived a young girl named Riya. Riya has a special gift, an extraordinary one. She had a special connection with nature and always found wonder in the smallest of things.

As Diwali, the Festival of Lights, approached, Riya's heart was filled with anticipation and happiness. She loved the vibrant decorations, the delicious sweets, and, most of all, the warm glow of countless diyas that adorned the village and brought smiles to anyone who looked at it. This year, Riya had a unique wish.

Riya wished to witness a sight that had only been whispered about in stories—the legendary "Dancing Fireflies of Diwali." These fireflies were said to come out only during Diwali, creating a magical spectacle that filled the night sky with a mesmerizing dance of tiny lights.

Riya and the Dancing Fireflies

On the eve of Diwali, Riya's grandmother, Nani, shared a story with her. It was the tale of a kind-hearted girl named Maya, much like Riya herself.

Maya had a deep love for nature and wished to witness the Dancing Fireflies of Diwali. One evening, as she wandered into the forest, she saw a glimmering light in the distance. Drawn by curiosity, she followed it.

To her amazement, the light led her to a grove filled with fireflies, their tiny bodies glowing like stars. As Maya watched, the fireflies began to dance in perfect harmony, creating a breathtaking spectacle that lit up the entire forest.

Nani's story filled Riya's heart with hope and excitement. That night, as the village celebrated Diwali, Riya made her way to a quiet spot near the forest, clutching a small diya in her hand.

She closed her eyes and made a silent wish - to witness the Dancing Fireflies of Diwali.

Riya and the Dancing Fireflies

As she lit the diya, its warm light joined the flickering lamps of the village, creating a tapestry of twinkling stars.

Suddenly, Riya heard a soft, melodious hum. She opened her eyes to find herself surrounded by a breathtaking dance of fireflies, just like in Nani's story. The tiny lights twirled and danced, casting a magical glow all around.

Riya felt like she was in a dream, her heart brimming with joy. She knew that her wish had come true, and she had been granted a glimpse of the Dancing Fireflies of Diwali.

As Riya returned home, her heart aglow with wonder, she knew that Diwali was not just about lights; it was about the magic that surrounds us when we open our hearts to the beauty of the world.

With that magical memory in her heart, Riya drifted off to sleep, her dreams filled with the enchanting dance of the fireflies. And as she slept, the village sparkled with the light of love, joy, and the timeless magic of Diwali.

CHAPTER NINE

The Magical Fireflies

Once upon a time, in a small village nestled by a serene river, there lived a boy named Rohan. Rohan was known for his warm heart and bright smile and everyone adored him. On the day of Diwali, after the family celebrations, he found himself feeling lost and lonely. His family had gone to visit relatives, and he was left behind, feeling like a solitary star in the dark sky.

As the sun dipped below the horizon, bored of staying alone, Rohan wandered into the forest. The forest was calmly quietand the gentle rustling of leaves and the distant sound of laughter filled the air. It was Diwali, the festival of lights, and the entire village was adorned with lanterns and candles. But for Rohan, it only emphasized his loneliness.

Tears welled up in his eyes as he walked deeper into the forest until he stumbled upon a clearing aglow with the soft, magical light of fireflies. These were no ordinary fireflies; they were young and mischievous, and are called the "Glimmering Glee."

The Magical Fireflies

Curious about the little boy, they fluttered around him, forming intricate patterns with their lights. One of them, a firefly named Luna, landed on Rohan's shoulder and asked, "Why do you look so sad, young one?"

Rohan wiped away his tears and explained his predicament. Luna and her friends, Spark, Ember, and Glow, decided to help him. They began to dance in the air, creating a mesmerizing display of light. Rohan couldn't help but smile as their radiant dance filled his heart with joy.

With their guidance, Rohan realized that Diwali was not just about lights and lanterns but about sharing happiness with others. He decided to spread the joy he had found with those who needed it the most.

Together, Rohan and the fireflies visited the elderly, lit up the homes of the less fortunate, and helped families reconnect with each other. As they shared their light, they saw faces light up with gratitude and happiness.

The Magical Fireflies

When the night came to an end, Rohan returned to his village, no longer feeling lonely. He had learned the true essence of Diwali - spreading light and happiness to others. The magical fireflies illuminated his heart, teaching him that the real magic of the festival was in the joy he brought to others.

From that day on, Rohan and the Glimmering Glee fireflies were inseparable, and every Diwali, they joined together to light up the lives of all who needed it, reminding everyone that the light of kindness and love was the most magical light of all.

CHAPTER TEN

A Festival of Friendship

In a peaceful village nestled between rolling hills, there was a unique and heartwarming tradition that celebrated the spirit of friendship. This special festival was known as the "Festival of Friendship," and it was a time when the entire village would come together to honor the bonds of companionship and kindness.

The festival is always celebrated on the eve of Diwali, the Festival of Lights, and it holdsa special place in the hearts of the villagers. The festival's main tradition involved exchanging handmade friendship bracelets, each one a symbol of the cherished bonds between friends.

In this village lived a young girl named Aanya, who had a gift for creating the most beautiful friendship bracelets. Aanya had friends from all walks of life, and she cherished every one of them. She believed that friendship was like a shining light that brightened even the darkest days.

A Festival of Friendship

As the Festival of Friendship approached, Aanya worked tirelessly to create the most exquisite bracelets for her friends. Each one was unique, reflecting the personality and interests of the recipient. She couldn't wait to see the joy on her friends' faces as they received her heartfelt gifts.

On the eve of the festival, the village square transformed into a vibrant and colorful gathering. Friends exchanged bracelets, hugged, and shared stories. The air was filled with laughter and the sweet aroma of traditional sweets.

As Aanya handed out her handmade bracelets to her friends, their eyes sparkled with appreciation. Each bracelet was a symbol of their enduring friendship, a reminder that they were cherished and valued.

As the evening drew to a close, Aanya looked around at the smiling faces and felt her heart swell with happiness.

A Festival of Friendship

The "Festival of Friendship" had once again filled the village with the warmth of love and camaraderie.

That night, as Aanya lay in her cozy bed, she knew that friendship was a treasure beyond measure, something to be celebrated and cherished. With a heart full of gratitude, she drifted off to sleep, her dreams filled with the joy of the "Festival of Friendship." And as she slept, the village glowed with the light of friendship, kindness, and the timeless celebration of bonds that would last a lifetime.

CHAPTER ELEVEN

Gopal's Diwali Delicacies

In a lively village named SundarNagar, nestled amidst lush green fields, there lived a young boy named Gopal. Just like every young boy of his age, Gopal was curious and also really smart. He had a special talent that made everyone adore him and made him the talk of the town—his extraordinary ability to create the most delicious Diwali delicacies.

As Diwali, the Festival of Lights, approached, Gopal's heart filled with excitement and anticipation. It wasn't the twinkling lights or the colorful decorations that thrilled him the most, but the opportunity to share his culinary creations with the village.

In the days leading up to Diwali, Gopal spent days in his grandmother's kitchen, perfecting recipes that had been passed down through generations. He baked crispy jalebis that melted in your mouth, fragrant gulab jamuns that were like sweet clouds, and savory samosas that were the perfect blend of spices and flavors.

Gopal's Diwali Delicacies

But Gopal's pièce de résistance was his secret recipe for the most delectable Diwali sweets. He called them "Diwali Delicacies," and they were unlike anything anyone had ever tasted. Each sweet was a miniature work of art, adorned with intricate designs and vibrant colors.

Finally, Diwali came and Gopal excitedly packed his goodies into his boxes, waiting for the right time to unbox them and unveil his unique creations to the village.

On the night of Diwali, Gopal set up a small stall in the village square, displaying his mouthwatering creations. The villagers gathered around, their mouths watering at the sight of the delicious treats.

Immediately they took their first bites, the villagers couldn't help but sigh with delight. Gopal's Diwali Delicacies were a symphony of flavors, a celebration of the sweetness of life. They brought smiles and warmth to everyone's hearts.

Gopal's Diwali Delicacies

People from all corners of the village came to taste Gopal's sweets, and they couldn't get enough. They praised his culinary skills and showered him with gratitude for making their Diwali extra special.

Gopal was overwhelmed with happiness, knowing that he had added a dash of magic to their celebrations. He realized that Diwali wasn't just about lights; it was about the light that shines from the hearts of those who share their love and talents with others.

That night, as Gopal lay in his cozy bed, he knew that his Diwali Delicacies had brought joy and togetherness to the village. With a heart full of contentment, he drifted off to sleep, his dreams filled with the sweet memories of Diwali. As he slept, the village glowed with the light of love, unity, and the timeless tradition of sharing during the Festival of Lights.

CHAPTER TWELVE

Diwali Dreams: Tales of Twinkling Lights

Once upon a time, in a charming village named Sundarapur, there lived a young boy named Raj. Raj loved Diwali more than any other festival. It was a time when the entire village sparkled with joy and laughter.

Every evening, Raj would sit with Meera and tell her stories about Diwali. He called them "Diwali Dreams: Tales of Twinkling Lights." These stories were magical, filled with wonder and enchantment.

One night, Raj began a new story. "Meera," he said, "tonight's story is about a curious firefly named Lumi." Lumi lived in a dense forest near Sundarapur. While all the other fireflies were content to light up the forest with their tiny glows, Lumi dreamt of something bigger. She wanted to shine as brightly as the Diwali lights that adorned their village.

Diwali Dreams: Tales of Twinkling Lights

One Diwali eve, as Lumi watched the village from afar, she spotted a flickering light that was brighter than all the others. It was the village's grand Diwali lamp, placed at the center of the celebrations. Lumi decided that she wanted to shine as brilliantly as that lamp.

With determination in her heart, Lumi set off on an adventure. She flew to the village square and approached the Diwali lamp. The lamp, sensing her earnest desire, whispered, "Lumi, you have a special light within you. To shine brightly, you must share your light with others."

Lumi understood the lamp's wisdom. She flew back to the forest and shared her glow with all the fireflies. As they glowed together, their combined light illuminated the entire forest, making it as radiant as the Diwali village.

Meera listened intently to the story, her eyes filled with wonder.

Diwali Dreams: Tales of Twinkling Lights

Raj concluded, "You see, Meera, Diwali is not just about lights; it's about the light of love, kindness, and togetherness. Like Lumi, we can all shine brightly by sharing our light with others."

With those words, Raj and Meera drifted off to sleep, their hearts warmed by the magic of Diwali Dreams, where twinkling lights of love and compassion illuminated their dreams.

CHAPTER THIRTEEN

Ananya's Magical Monkey

In a lush forest, there lived a mischievous little monkey named Ananya. She was known throughout the jungle for her boundless curiosity and love for adventure. Ananya's favorite time of the year was Diwali, the Festival of Lights.

As Diwali approached, Ananya's heart was filled with excitement. She watched the animals in the forest prepare for the celebration, decorating their homes with colorful flowers and leaves. Ananya couldn't wait to join in the festivities, but she wanted to do something special for her friends.

One day, as she swung through the trees, she met a wise old owl named Hoot. Ananya shared her desire to make Diwali magical for her friends. Hoot listened intently and then told her about a legend—a legend of the "Magical Diwali Stars."

Ananya's Magical Monkey

According to the legend, on Diwali night, special stars would descend from the sky, carrying the hopes and dreams of all the forest animals. These stars had the power to make wishes come true.

Ananya's eyes sparkled with excitement. She knew what she had to do. She spent days crafting tiny paper stars, each one filled with a heartfelt wish for her friends—a cozy nest for Squeaky the squirrel, a shiny new shell for Shelly the turtle, and a delicious fruit tree for Timmy the rabbit.

On the night of Diwali, Ananya placed her paper stars in a basket and climbed the tallest tree in the jungle. With all her might, she tossed the basket into the sky. The stars twinkled as they soared higher and higher, carrying Ananya's wishes into the night.

As the stars reached the heavens, they transformed into shimmering constellations that lit up the jungle. Ananya's friends watched in awe as the night sky sparkled with their wishes.

Ananya's Magical Monkey

The jungle came alive with the sounds of laughter and joy as the animals realized that their dreams were coming true. Squeaky had a cozy nest, Shelly a shiny new shell, and Timmy a fruit tree filled with delicious treats.

Ananya's Magical Diwali had made their dreams come true. She had shown that Diwali was not just about lights but about the light of love, kindness, and the magic of making wishes for others.

That night, as Ananya curled up in her cozy tree branch, she knew that she had created a Diwali to remember. With a heart full of contentment, she drifted off to sleep, her dreams illuminated by the warm, twinkling memories of Ananya's Magical Diwali. And as she slept, the jungle glowed with the light of friendship, happiness, and the timeless magic of the festival.

CHAPTER FOURTEEN

The Diwali Starry Night

Maya loved the vibrant decorations, the delicious sweets, and the warm glow of countless diyas that adorned her village.

This year's Diwali was just a few days away, but there was a problem. The village's precious diya supply had run out, and there were none left to light. The villagers were heartbroken, and the festive spirit began to fade.

Maya, a determined and resourceful girl, couldn't bear to see her village in such despair. She decided to embark on a journey to find the most magical diya ever known—the "Diwali Starry Night Diya." It was said to possess the power to light up the entire village with a single flame.

With a small lantern in her hand, Maya bravely set off into the moonlit night. She ventured through forests, crossed meandering streams, and climbed steep hills, guided only by the stars and her unwavering determination.

The Diwali Starry Night

After days of searching, she stumbled upon a mystical grove deep in the heart of the forest. There, under the ancient banyan tree, she discovered the fabled "Diwali Starry Night Diya." It was unlike any diya she had ever seen, with intricate designs that sparkled like stars themselves.

Maya carefully lit the diya, and as its flame flickered to life, something extraordinary happened. The entire grove began to glow with a warm, golden light. Maya realized that she had found the diya that could save Diwali for her village.

With the "Diwali Starry Night Diya" in her lantern, Maya hurried back to the village. As she approached, the villagers saw the radiant glow emanating from her lantern and rushed to welcome her.

Maya placed the diya in the center of the village square, and with a single flame, it lit up the entire village.

The Diwali Starry Night

The warm, golden light spread to every corner, and the village was bathed in a breathtaking glow that was brighter and more magical than ever before.

Maya's courage and determination had saved Diwali. The villagers cheered and celebrated, their hearts filled with gratitude for the little girl who had brought back the festive spirit.

That night, as Maya lay in her cozy bed, she knew that Diwali was not just about lights but about the light of hope, determination, and the magic of never giving up. With a contented heart, she drifted off to sleep, her dreams illuminated by the warm, twinkling memories of The Diwali Starry Night. And as she slept, the village glowed with the light of unity, happiness, and the timeless magic of the festival.

CHAPTER FIFTEEN

Moonlight Adventures

There was a young boy named Raj who was known throughout his village for his boundless imagination and his love for Diwali, the Festival of Lights. Every year, he looked forward to the colorful decorations, the delicious sweets, and the warm glow of countless diyas that lit up the village.

One Diwali eve, as Raj gazed at the radiant moon in the night sky, a wild idea struck him. He wondered if the moon itself could be a part of the Diwali celebrations. He thought of it for a while and decided to embark on a magical adventure—the "Diwali Moonlight Adventures."

Raj climbed up the tallest hill in the village, carrying a paper lantern in his hand. He believed that if he could reach the moon, he could bring back its silvery light to make Diwali even more special.

Moonlight Adventures

As he reached the summit, Raj released his lantern into the night sky. He watched with awe as it soared higher and higher, disappearing into the velvety darkness. He felt like he had sent a piece of his heart to the moon.

To his astonishment, the moon seemed to respond. It cast a silvery beam of light that touched Raj's lantern, making it glow even brighter. The moonlight danced with his lantern's light, creating a mesmerizing display.

Raj knew he had to share this magic with his village. He raced back to Chandrapur and gathered the villagers in the square. With their lanterns in hand, they looked up at the moon, and Raj's lantern lit up with the moonlight once again.

The village square came alive with the enchanting glow of the "Diwali Moonlight Adventures." It was a sight that filled the villagers' hearts with wonder and joy. Raj had succeeded in making the moon a part of their Diwali celebration.

Moonlight Adventures

As the night continued, the moonlight illuminated the village, creating a serene and magical atmosphere. The villagers danced and sang, their hearts lifted by the enchantment of the night.

That night, as Raj lay in his cozy bed, he knew that Diwali was not just about lights but about the light of imagination, adventure, and the magic that lies within each of us. With a contented heart, he drifted off to sleep, his dreams illuminated by the warm, silvery memories of The Diwali Moonlight Adventures. And as he slept, the village glowed with the light of creativity, joy, and the timeless magic of the festival.

Dear Readers,

Our team would like to thank you sincerely for purchasing our book Diwali Bedtime Stories. Your support and interest in our work are extremely important and inspiring to us.

Your feedback is valuable to us, so We would like to ask you to share your thoughts about the book on the Amazon platform. Your honest reviews will help us better understand what your opinion is about our book and what elements can be improved or changed in the future.

We greatly appreciate every comment, whether it is positive or negative. Your feedback will help other readers make an informed choice when purchasing a book.

Once again, thank you for your support and for choosing our Diwali Bedtime Stories. We hope you enjoyed the story and provided moments of relaxation and joy.

Best regards,

Team Devan B. Sharma

Printed in Great Britain
by Amazon

31072908R00030